D1001449

POWER TRACTORS

by **Michael Williams**

PUBLISHING

A Member of the WRC Media Family of Companies

Please visit our Web site at: **www.garethstevens.com**
For a free color catalog describing Gareth Stevens Publishing's
list of high-quality books and multimedia programs,
call 1-800-542-2595 (USA) or 1-800-387-3178 (Canada).
Gareth Stevens Publishing's fax: (414) 332-3567.

Library of Congress Cataloging-in-Publication Data

Williams, Michael, 1935-
  Power tractors / Michael Williams.
      p. cm. — (Cool wheels)
  Includes bibliographical references and index.
  ISBN-10: 0-8368-6828-5 – ISBN-13: 978-0-8368-6828-9 (lib. bdg.)
  1. Tractors—History—Juvenile literature. I. Title. II. Series
TL233.15.W54   2006
629.225'2—dc22   2006042292

This North American edition first published in 2007 by
Gareth Stevens Publishing
A Member of the WRC Media Family of Companies
330 West Olive Street, Suite 100
Milwaukee, WI 53212 USA

© 2006 Amber Books Ltd.

Produced by Amber Books Ltd., Bradley's Close,
74–77 White Lion Street, London N1 9PF, U.K.

Project Editor: Michael Spilling
Design: SOL
Picture Research: Terry Forshaw and Kate Green

Gareth Stevens editorial direction: Valerie J. Weber
Gareth Stevens editor: Jim Mezzanotte
Gareth Stevens art direction: Tammy West
Gareth Stevens cover design: Charlie Dahl
Gareth Stevens production: Jessica Morris

Picture credits: Michael Williams: 5, 7, 9, 11, 13, 17, 19, 23, 27; Ag-Chem Europe B.V.: 15;
Buhler Industries Inc: 21; New Holland: 25; Massey Ferguson (AGCO Corporation): 29.

Artwork credits: John Deere: 4; Mark Franklin (© Amber Books): 6, 12, 14, 16, 18, 20, 24, 26, 28;
Amber Books: 8, 22; Michael Williams (Caterpillar): 10; Terex Mining: 26.

We would also like to thank the following manufacturers who sent us reference material for artwork images: FENDT (AGCO Corporation);
Ag-Chem Europe B.V.; Case IH; Massey Ferguson (AGCO Corporation); Buhler Industries Inc; New Holland; Deere & Company.

Printed in the United States of America

1 2 3 4 5 6 7 8 9 10 09 08 07 06

CONTENTS

JOHN DEERE MODEL D

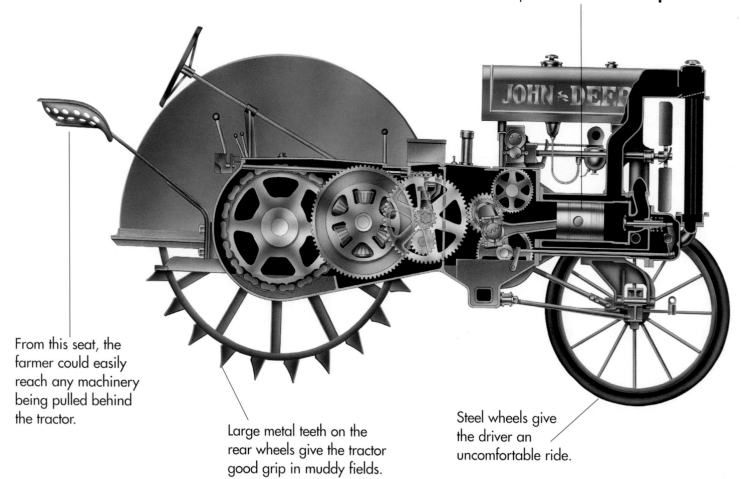

The engine has only two **cylinders**. It does not produce a lot of **horsepower**.

From this seat, the farmer could easily reach any machinery being pulled behind the tractor.

Large metal teeth on the rear wheels give the tractor good grip in muddy fields.

Steel wheels give the driver an uncomfortable ride.

The Model D is one of the most important tractors ever built. It is the first tractor that John Deere, the famous tractor maker, sold to farmers. It was very popular. Farmers liked the simple two-cylinder engine, which was easy to repair. With fewer engine parts to wear out or break, the Model D was more reliable than other tractors at the time.

JOHN DEERE MODEL D

First Year Made: 1923
Country of Tractor Maker: United States
Job: Pulling trailers and other machinery
Power: 30 horsepower

A Successful Machine
The first Model D tractors were built in 1923. They became so popular that they were made for thirty more years, until 1953.

For the older models, John Deere increased the tractor's power and improved it in other ways. The company sold more than 160,000 Model D tractors.

DID YOU KNOW?

The old John Deere two-cylinder engine made a "pop-pop" noise. It earned the nickname "Johnny Popper."

ALLIS-CHALMERS MODEL U

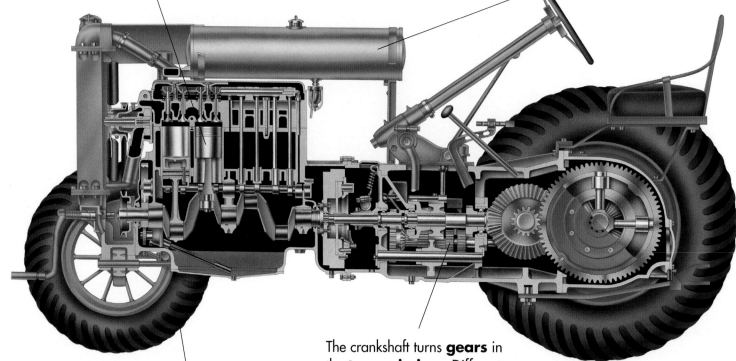

Pistons in the cylinders move up and down, turning the **crankshaft**. It sends power to the wheels.

Allis-Chalmers tractors have always been painted bright orange.

Rubber tires give a smoother ride than steel wheels.

The crankshaft turns **gears** in the **transmission**. Different gears let the tractor travel at different speeds.

The Allis-Chalmers Model U was first made in 1929. In 1932, it became the first tractor to use rubber tires filled with air.

Rolling Rubber

At first, the company replaced the tractor's steel wheels with wheels from an airplane. These wheels had rubber tires. The company soon found

that rubber tires did less damage to fields and roads.

The tires allowed the tractor to go faster, and they gave the driver a smoother ride. Soon, other tractor companies were also using rubber tires on their machines, and metal wheels became a thing of the past.

Left: Rubber tires allowed tractors to move faster and more smoothly over farm fields.

DID YOU KNOW?

Allis-Chalmers also built a special racing version of the Model U. At the Utah salt flats in 1933, it set a world speed record for tractors, reaching 67 miles (108 kilometers) per hour.

VERSATILE 256 BI-DI

This tractor can travel at the same speed both forward and backward.

The seat, steering wheel, and other controls can all turn around to face in the opposite direction.

The front and rear wheels are exactly the same size.

The tractor uses a **diesel** engine. It runs on diesel fuel instead of gasoline.

Left: This Versatile 256 is being driven forward to plow a field.

The Versatile 256 is a "two-way" tractor. It can work just as easily going backward as forward. It is also called bi-directional, or "Bi-Di."

Forward or Backward?
On this tractor, the seat and some of the controls are on a platform that can turn around to face the rear. Turning around makes it easier to use machinery on the back of the tractor, such as a loading shovel. Turning to face the rear is more comfortable than twisting around in the seat to see what is happening behind you. Facing backward is also useful for work where there is little space to turn the tractor around.

VERSATILE 256 BI-DI

First Year Made: 1984
Country of Tractor Maker: Canada
Job: General purpose, including loader work
Power: 100 horsepower

DID YOU KNOW?

This tractor has a special transmission. It allows the driver to go faster or slower without changing the speed of the engine.

CATERPILLAR CHALLENGER 65

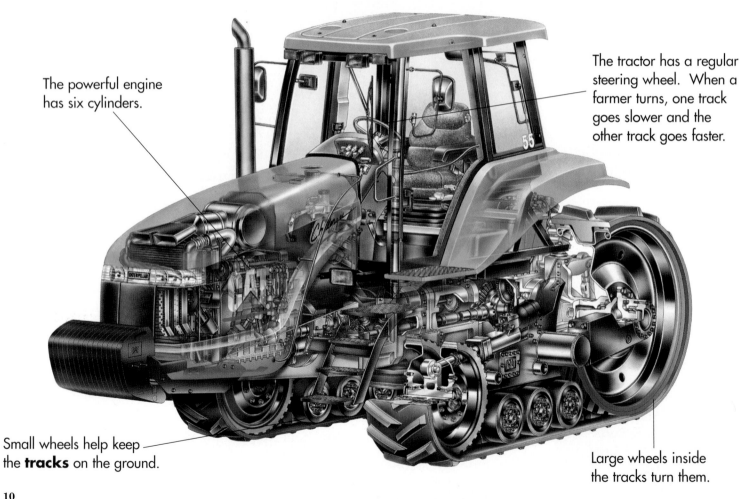

The powerful engine has six cylinders.

The tractor has a regular steering wheel. When a farmer turns, one track goes slower and the other track goes faster.

Small wheels help keep the **tracks** on the ground.

Large wheels inside the tracks turn them.

The Caterpillar Challenger 65 does not have regular wheels. Instead, each side has a belt called a track. The tracks are made of rubber. They have steel cables inside for strength. The engine turns a big wheel in each track. The wheels turn the tracks, making the tractor move.

Tracks are often used on soft ground. They do

Left: Like many tractors, the Challenger 65 has lights. Farmers can work early in the morning or at night, when it is dark.

not sink into the soil and compact it.

New Tracks
The Challenger 65 was the first tractor to use rubber tracks. Before it, all tracks were made of steel. Tractors with rubber tracks can travel on paved roads without damaging the surface. The rubber tracks also allow the tractor to go much faster.

Today, many other companies make tractors with rubber tracks.

CATERPILLAR CHALLENGER 65

First Year Made: 1987
Country of Tractor Maker: United States
Job: Pulling big **cultivators** and **seed drills**
Power: 270 horsepower

DID YOU KNOW?

These tracks are very strong. They have steel **cables** inside, so they will not break.

11

FENDT VARIO 926

The transmission in this tractor will change speeds automatically, but farmers can also change them by pushing buttons.

The Vario has **cruise control**. A farmer sets it to make the tractor always travel at a certain speed.

The six-cylinder engine produces 260 horsepower, which is a lot for a tractor.

The Fendt Vario 926 has a constantly variable transmission, or CVT. Transmissions on tractors usually have different gears. Farmers have to change gears as they ride. By changing gears, they change the tractor's speed but keep the engine speed about the same. With the 926, farmers can travel at whatever speeds they want, but there are no gears to change.

FENDT VARIO 926

First Year Made: 1994
**Country of Tractor
Maker:** Germany
Job: Pulling big machines
Power: 260 horsepower

Computer Control
The Vario 926 has a computer that controls the transmission.

Farmers do not have to think about changing gears. They can focus on their work instead.

DID YOU KNOW?

The Fendt Vario 926 took many years of planning. It is the first tractor in the world to have CVT. Today, many other tractor makers also offer CVT for their tractors.

TERRA-GATOR 8103

The container behind the cabin carries a load of fertilizer for spraying.

The tractor can spray **fertilizer** from these special tubes fitted to the side.

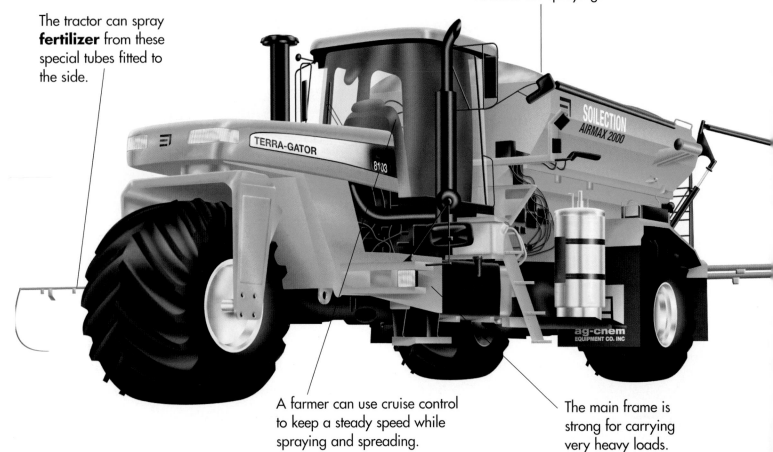

A farmer can use cruise control to keep a steady speed while spraying and spreading.

The main frame is strong for carrying very heavy loads.

Left: The Terra-Gator has huge tires. They help spread its weight and reduce the damage it might do to the soil.

Terra-Gators are used for special jobs. They spread and spray materials, such as fertilizer. Fertilizer helps plants grow.

A Tractor or a Truck?
The Terra-Gator is a cross between a tractor and a truck. Like a tractor, it can travel over rough ground. Like a truck, it can carry a heavy load.

The Terra-Gator is powerful, and it works fast. It has three wheels instead of four, so it is easier to turn at the edge of a field.

TERRA-GATOR 8103
First Year Made: 1997
Country of Tractor Maker: United States
Job: Spraying and spreading
Power: 300 horsepower

DID YOU KNOW?

The big "balloon" tires on the Terra-Gator are softer and more flexible than car or truck tires. With these tires, the tractor does not leave ruts in the soil. It is also less likely to get stuck.

CASE IH MAGNUM 285

Big windows in the cabin provide a good view from the driver's seat.

The engine has a **turbocharger** for more power.

The Magnum is easy to turn in a small space.

With "creeper" gears in its transmission, the tractor can travel at very slow speeds.

Since the 1980s, Case IH has increased the power of the Magnum tractors, and the 285 is the most powerful model so far. Farmers like the extra power. With this power, tractors can pull bigger machines and do jobs more quickly.

Bigger and Faster
Farmers are now using bigger machines that can work faster. Tractors such as the Magnum 285 give them the extra power they need to do more work in a shorter time. The latest Magnums have turbocharged engines. The tractors also have a better steering system, so they need less space to turn around.

Left: Magnum tractors are used mainly for plowing big fields.

CASE IH MAGNUM 285
First Year Made: 2002
Country of Tractor Maker: United States
Job: Plowing fields
Power: 315 horsepower

DID YOU KNOW?

How popular is the Case IH Magnum? Just one factory, in Basildon, England, has built more than 100,000 tractors!

MASSEY FERGUSON 6270

The driver sits in an enclosed cabin. It has heating and can also have air conditioning. Drivers can stay comfortable in all kinds of weather.

The **exhaust** stack is on the side, so it does not block the driver's view.

A special system helps stop the wheels from spinning on slippery ground.

Farmers use steps to reach the driver's seat, which is high off the ground.

Massey Ferguson tractors were the first tractors to use equipment that receives signals from **satellites** in space. The 6270 model has this equipment. It is useful for all kinds of farming jobs.

Space Age Tractors

These signals from space can show a farmer the exact position of a

Left: This tractor has thirty-two speeds. A farmer can easily find the best speed for the many different kinds of work the 6270 can do.

MASSEY FERGUSON 6270

First Year Made: 1999
Country of Tractor Maker: France
Job: General purpose
Power: 115 horsepower

tractor in the field. Knowing this position, the farmer can measure how far the tractor has traveled and how much work it has done. The farmer can then control how much fertilizer is spread on the field.

In the future, farmers may use satellite signals to steer "robot tractors." These tractors will not need drivers in them!

DID YOU KNOW?

The tractor's cabin can have a glass roof. If the tractor has a loader in front, a farmer is able to watch as the load is raised high.

BUHLER 2425

The 2425 has twelve gears for twelve different speeds. The driver selects speeds by pushing buttons.

A computer helps the engine produce cleaner exhaust, so it creates less **pollution**.

This tractor has **articulated steering**. Its front wheels do not turn. The tractor turns by bending in the midddle.

The huge engine gives the tractor a lot of pulling power.

Buhler is Canada's biggest tractor company. It is based in Winnipeg, Manitoba, where Versatile tractors used to be built.

Tractor Giants

The Buhler 2425 is a very large tractor that is used on big farms. Its engine turns all the wheels, giving it good grip. This tractor can pull the widest and

BUHLER 2425
First Year Made: 2000
Country of Tractor Maker: Canada
Job: Pulling machines on big farms
Power: 425 horsepower

heaviest machines. It has extra wheels for jobs such as plowing. The many wheels spread its weight, so it does not damage the soil.

The tractor's front wheels do not steer the tractor. Instead, the whole tractor bends in the middle when the steering wheel is turned.

DID YOU KNOW?

This tractor uses **aftercooling**, a system that cools the fuel. When the fuel is colder, more of it can go into the engine. More fuel creates more power.

CASE IH STEIGER STX440

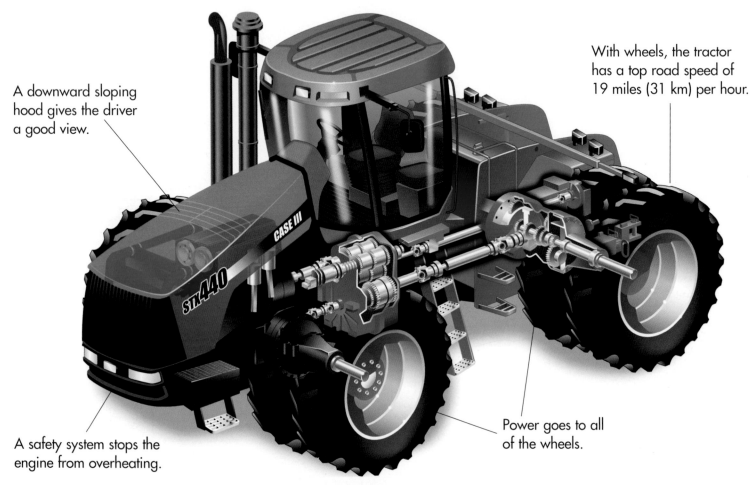

A downward sloping hood gives the driver a good view.

With wheels, the tractor has a top road speed of 19 miles (31 km) per hour.

A safety system stops the engine from overheating.

Power goes to all of the wheels.

Steiger STX tractors come with wheels or Quadtrac. An STX

CASE IH STEIGER STX440

First Year Made: 2000
Country of Tractor
  Maker: United States
Job: Pulling heavy machinery
Power: 440 horsepower

with Quadtrac has four rubber tracks — one at each corner.

Traveling on Tracks

With four wide tracks, an STX has a lot of rubber gripping the ground, for extra pulling

power. The tracks also spread the tractor's weight over a large area. The tractor can travel on soft ground without sinking, and it does not compact the soil. Crops grow poorly when the soil has been pressed down.

NEW HOLLAND TG 285

The cabin is large, so the driver has room to work comfortably.

The rear **linkage** is strong enough to pull a machine weighing more than 7 tons.

The **suspension** gives the driver a smooth ride.

Creeper gears in the transmission allow the tractor to travel very slowly, which is useful for harvesting crops.

On modern farms, farmers need powerful tractors that can do more work in less time. The TG 285 has more power than earlier New Holland tractors.

An Efficient Engine
An electronic system sends exactly the right amount of fuel to the cylinders of the TG 285 engine. This system is very **efficient**. The engine does not waste fuel, and it easy for the driver to use.

NEW HOLLAND TG 285

First Year Made: 2002
Country of Tractor Maker: England
Job: Harvesting
Power: 283 horsepower

DID YOU KNOW?

The TG 285 can be fitted with steering that guides the tractor across the field in a straight line, making the farmer's job easier.

JOHN DEERE 9620

The six-cylinder, PowerTech engine is built at the John Deere factory in Iowa.

The cabin has an extra seat for carrying a passenger.

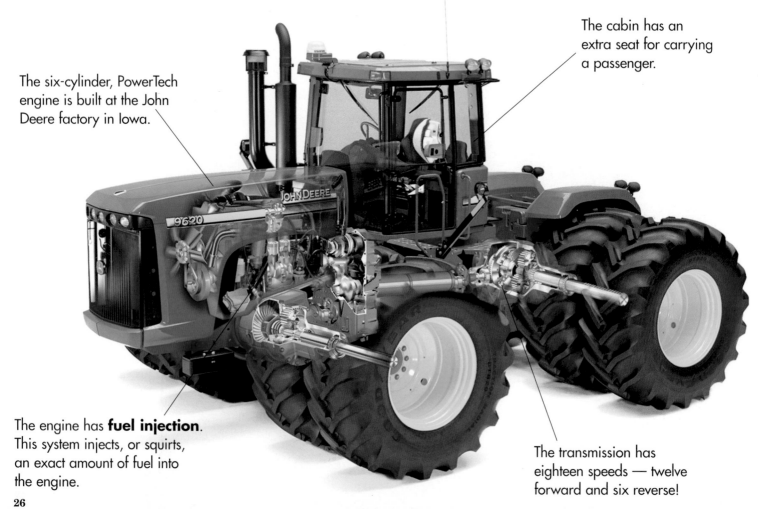

The engine has **fuel injection**. This system injects, or squirts, an exact amount of fuel into the engine.

The transmission has eighteen speeds — twelve forward and six reverse!

The 9620 is the most powerful tractor John Deere has ever built. It is designed for very large farms that grow many acres (hectares) of crops.

Hard-Working Tractors

On big farms, machines such as planters and cultivators can do their jobs in a short time and over a large area. These machines must be pulled

Left: The 9620 is painted in green and yellow, just like other John Deere tractors. These colors date back to the first John Deere tractors of the 1920s.

JOHN DEERE 9620

First Year Made: 2004
Country of Tractor Maker: United States
Job: Pulling heavy machinery on large farms
Power: 535 horsepower

by powerful tractors. The John Deere 9620 is expensive, but it helps farmers do a lot of work. With it, farmers can plant and harvest crops at the right time.

Night Worker

The 9620 can work at night as well as during the day. High-powered lights can be fitted to the tractor to provide a bright, clear view.

DID YOU KNOW?

Like earlier John Deere tractors, the 9620 can also be fitted with rubber tracks.

MASSEY FERGUSON 8480

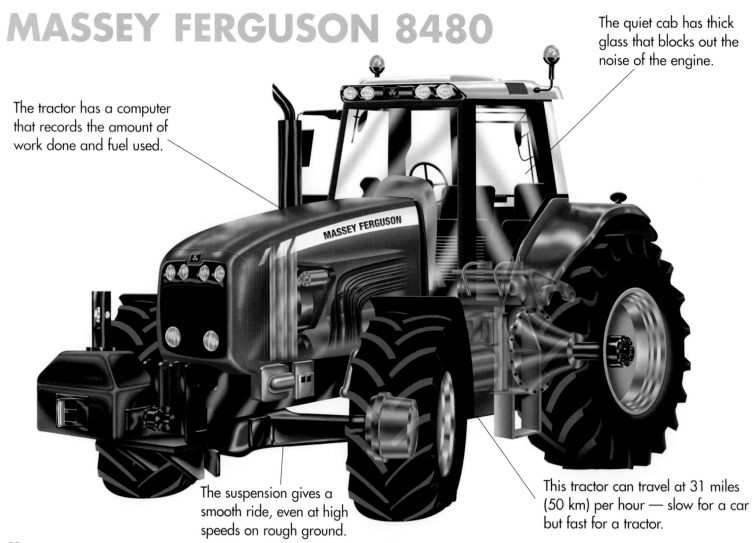

The quiet cab has thick glass that blocks out the noise of the engine.

The tractor has a computer that records the amount of work done and fuel used.

The suspension gives a smooth ride, even at high speeds on rough ground.

This tractor can travel at 31 miles (50 km) per hour — slow for a car but fast for a tractor.

The Massey Ferguson 8400 series is made by AGCO, one of the biggest tractor makers in the world. AGCO is based in the United States, but its tractors are made in France.

MASSEY FERGUSON 8480

First Year Made: 2004
Country of Tractor
 Maker: France
Job: Pulling heavy machinery
Power: 315 horsepower

A Different Fuel

The 8400 series tractors can use biodiesel for fuel. Regular diesel is made from **petroleum**, just like gasoline. Biodiesel is made from crops, such as wheat, soybean, or sugar cane. As the world's oil supplies run out, people may start using biodiesel in cars.

DID YOU KNOW?

In the "economy" setting, the control system automatically keeps the engine speed as slow as possible to avoid wasting fuel.

GLOSSARY

aftercooling — a system that cools fuel so that more of it goes into an engine, producing more power.

articulated steering — a special steering system. With this system, a tractor's front wheels do not turn. The front and back parts of the tractor are on a hinge, so the tractor turns by bending in the middle.

cables — metal ropes made of strands of wire.

crankshaft — the part of an engine that connects to the pistons. It spins around when the pistons move up and down inside the cylinders.

cruise control — a system that keeps a tractor moving at a constant speed. This speed is set by the farmer.

cultivators — machines that break up soil to help plants grow.

cylinders — spaces inside an engine where fuel and air explode to create power.

diesel — the name for a kind of engine and the special fuel it uses. Most diesel engines are very reliable.

efficient — able to do something without wasting energy.

exhaust — the gases an engine creates when it burns fuel and air.

fertilizer — something added to soil to help plants grow.

fuel injection — a system that sprays fuel into an engine.

gears — small, toothed wheels. The many gears in a tractor's transmission allow it to travel at different speeds.

horsepower — the amount of power an engine makes, based on how much work one horse can do.

linkage — the part of a tractor that attaches to different machines the tractor pulls, such as plows and cultivators.

petroleum — a liquid found deep in the ground that can be made into fuels, such as gasoline and diesel. It is also called oil.

pistons — metal tubes inside an engine's cylinders that move up and down when fuel and air explodes, turning the crankshaft.

pollution — waste from factories and vehicles that is harmful to people and the environment.

satellites — machines that orbit, or circle, Earth in space. They can take photographs and send information.

seed drills — machines that puts seeds into the soil.

suspension — the parts that attach the wheels to a tractor and help it ride smoothly on bumpy surfaces.

tracks — rubber or metal belts that circle around a row of wheels to move a vehicle, such as a tractor.

transmission — the part of a tractor that sends the spinning power of the engine's crankshaft to the wheels.

turbocharger — a machine that pumps extra air into an engine for more power. It spins from the force of exhaust gases leaving the engine.

FOR MORE INFORMATION

Books

Farm Tractors. Mighty Movers (series).
  Sarah Tieck (Buddy Books)

Farm Tractors. Pull Ahead Transportation (series).
  Kristin L. Nelson (Lerner Publishing Group)

Tractor. Machines at Work (series).
  Caroline Bingham (DK Publishing)

Tractors. Big Machines (series).
  David Glover and Penny Glover (Smart Apple Media)

Tractors. Transportation (series). Darlene R. Stille
  (Compass Point Books)

Tremendous Tractors. Amazing Machines (series).
  Tony Mitton (Kingfisher)

Web Sites

Big Tractor Power
www.bigtractorpower.com

Buhler: Tractors
www.buhler.com/products/tractor-main.shtml

Modern Farm Tractors
www.historylink101.com/lessons/farm-city/early-tractors.htm

Inventors — Tractors and Bulldozers
inventors.about.com/library/inventors/bltractor.htm

South Dakota State Agricultural Heritage Museum
www.agmuseum.com/exhibits.html

INDEX